SIX BAD POETS

Six Bad Poets

CHRISTOPHER REID

faber and faber

First published in 2013
by Faber and Faber Ltd
Bloomsbury House
74–77 Great Russell Street
London WCIB 3DA

Typeset by Faber and Faber Ltd
Printed in England by T. J. International Ltd, Padstow, Cornwall

A CIP record for this book is available from the British Library

ISBN 978–0–571–30403–5

2 4 6 8 10 9 7 5 3 1

I've half a mind to tumble down to prose,
But verse is more in fashion – so here goes.
   Byron, *Beppo*

Six Bad Poets ⟡

One ∿

I

Charles Prime, an old, forgotten poet,
is back in town after ten years away.
Two country marriages, plus a spell in gaol –
brief fling with Her Maj – explain the unnatural absence;
but now he's loping down Old Compton Street
in gingery hacking jacket and tight jeans.

Casting an eye on once-familiar scenes
turned not so, aloof, apart,
he won't stop long enough to stare at
anything, but like a fox, both hunter and possible prey,
sniffs at and notes in his nerves the escape options,
before spurting on to his true goal:

that light-shy, literary pub, the Agèd Eagle,
where Jimmy McDodd once swam in pink gins
like a seal, and P. T. Thurrock made sprawling obeisance
to a more nimbly fist-flinging poet
in the course of a row about Mallarmé.
May not be home, but it should give him a start . . .

Look at Charles: trim, fit as a stoat,
packed with élan vital and animal guile –
and seventy-seven years old, if he's a day!
Weather eye tuned to the main chance,
he's suffered a thousand setbacks, upsets, prat-
falls, yet aspires to keep faith with his juvenile ambitions.

The Eagle's crew of noonday apparitions
welcomes him in. 'Here, Charlie-boy! Going straight?'
some wag asks. He takes his usual, a gin and port,
which the known and friendly gargoyle
behind the bar has poured unprompted, with 'Keep the change!'
So far, touch wooden counter, OK.

Then: 'Charlie, some young poof was in just yesterday,
asking after you. Sent him about his business.'
'Young poof?' 'Yeah, bangles, pony-tail, all that monkeyshines.'
'Strange. Asked for me?' His manner is distrait.
'Weren't for his height, he could of been a girl.
Or some new-fangled poncy kind of pirate.'

2

Antonia Candling, doyenne of London poetry,
gazes across her broad, well-ordered desk
at the figure of her husband toiling up Primrose Hill.
Tubby, in tracksuit and trainers, he appears
to her, for a truant second, like a sniper's anonymous
mark. Pow! Then she cancels the image sharply.

Her own figure, at sixty, remains shapely,
and her face, she can honestly tell herself, rather pretty.
The Fates presiding at her birth must have felt magnanimous.
Yet how to account for the almost grotesque
contrast with Bernard: his complexion like plaster-of-Paris,
buck teeth, bald scalp, bulging midriff, bandy legs, and all?

In fact, it's been a happy match, on the whole,
and, while she's not one to look at these things soppily,
she blesses the evening when, as halves of different pairs,
they converged on the same bohemian party,
met, then went home with the pairs reshuffled. Tsk, tsk!
Their former partners are still their fiercest enemies.

She often has cause to reflect on the animus
her obvious good fortune rouses in others. Well,
let that be their problem; it's not her task
to redistribute the world's uneven supply
of luck, success, or money. Was there ever parity
in such matters? Take your complaints to the heavenly powers!

From a Lucie Rie jug, Antonia pours
fresh water into her Pleydell-Bouverie vase of anemones:
perfect taste in both flowers and pottery!
Not to mention the pictures on her wall.
Or, underfoot, the expanse of soberly
coloured kelims. Or the netsukes on her desk,

at which she sits in reverie till long after dusk,
forgetting to switch on the light, forgetting the prose –
book-jacket puff – she's meant to be writing, simply
letting time drift. But then an ominous
thought occurs: Bernard? His footsteps in the hall
are normally unmissable, audibly portly.

3

Jonathan Wilderness, a young poet on the make,
is sharing instant coffee and a joint
with his friend Baz, a self-employed criminal.
'Plans?' he says. 'Sure, I've got plans. You won't catch me
wasting my youth and beauty here.' With disgust,
he surveys the kitchen where they're sitting.

Distinctly foppish in this squalid setting,
where everything wears a tinge of grime and murk –
hard to say which is more heavily greased,
frying-pan or floor – he adds: 'No, I shan't
be more than a fortnight. End of May,
at the latest.' With a long and exquisite fingernail,

he picks at a scab of ketchup, all but annealed
to the table-top. 'That's for certain.
Then I'm off and away and you won't see me
for stardust.' 'Yeah,' Baz says, with a smirk;
'but the plan?' Jonathan keeps at his urgent,
fastidious work on the crimson crust

for a while, apparently too engrossed
to answer, till: 'Nothing's final,
you understand, but I've got this ancient,
clapped-out poet in my sights: a sitting
duck, you might say; fat, juicy, smack
in my line of fire – and just begging to have me

write his biography. Or so he will when he meets me.
Our paths haven't, as yet, actually crossed.
But when they do, there'll be plenty of muck
to rummage around in. Vintage quality. *Vinyl*.
A whole cart of bad apples, ready for upsetting.
Of course, I'll need a good, unscrupulous agent.'

A rangy girl strolls in, naked and nonchalant.
Jonathan frowns at her: 'Oh, Mimi,
must you?' Baz finds this fairly exciting,
but Jonathan's underjoyed: 'Not when we have a guest.
If you can't be arsed to put your clothes on, I'll . . .'
She yawns, turns about, and leaves, making no remark.

4

Derek Dufton, poet and academic,
wakes with a start and shudder from his sleep
in the middle of a lecture he is delivering
on 'Tennyson and le Néant'. So far
as he can tell from a glance at his meagre audience,
nobody has noticed. Nonetheless, he's worried,

and for the rest of the day remains worried.
Can he really have been spouting on automatic?
If so, for how many minutes? Hard evidence
is lacking, but a sense of the slippery slope
that every superior intellect must fear
pierces him and has him inwardly shivering.

At weakest moments, he feels himself dithering
on the edge of confiding in one of his less weird
department colleagues; but that would be a step too far.
Day-to-day dealings with them are at best problematic:
even admitting to a need for sleep
at night could look like the wildest decadence.

Impossible, of course, to speak to any of his students –
apart, perhaps, from Gail, whom he's been considering
making a play for, if only he knew how to slip
behind those defences: pretty, swotty, awkward,
unsmiling post-grad Gail, with her skin of ceramic
flawlessness and hair as gold and dense as the fur

of some legendary beast, who is therefore
untouchable and whom such a frank confidence
would merely bewilder. So, to the dismal tick
of his wall-clock, he sits, silently gibbering.
He can't work. Can't write a word.
Can't even – irony! – snatch a wink of sleep.

Received poetic wisdom about sleep
is scarcely encouraging: next thing to death and hellfire!
Our obsolescence being hard-wired,
when, as this morning, the truth calls, we dance
like marionettes to its music: a skeleton's fiddling
in a carnival caper we must not misread as comic.

5

Jane Steep, a poet still in search of her voice,
is on the night bus heading home from her shift
at Sunny's Kebab and Pizza Restaurant.
She has a book of poems in her bag,
but is too tired, too angry as well,
to get it out. She hates her job. She has to leave it.

The journey home itself is a horror. To brave it,
she must disregard all other passengers on the bus
and stare straight ahead, even while
the ghoul on her left is giving her the odd shove
with his elbow and a drunk at the back
is aiming grimaces her way. But she must be strong.

Only just out of uni, and everything's gone wrong,
she thinks, recoiling as some hulking halfwit
lurches into her. She uses her basketwork bag
as a flimsy shield, then feels for her purse:
still there, thank heaven – could have been a close shave.
The bus dawdles on towards Camberwell.

Tonight, her head's in a worse than usual whirl,
and her nerves, never less than highly strung,
are jangling like a harpsichord, all because the chef,
Kurdish Dave, who has fallen into the loutish habit
of pinching her bottom each time she passes,
finally drove her to answer back,

hitting him in the face with a catering pack
of frozen chips. You should have heard his wail!
'Is big crime!' he cried. 'I tell boss!'
But Sunny seemed more amused than otherwise, stirring
Dave's wrath further: 'I let you have it,
little girl, tomorrow.' And his look meant mischief.

So Jane sits, poking at a moth-hole in her scarf,
loosening the yarn. If only she could unpick
the past so easily! She feels like a rabbit
trying to make a dog disappear by an effort of will.
Exhausted, fearful and tearful, she sits staring
at South London's passing night lights and night blurs.

6

Bryony Butters, poet, novelist, and more besides,
has rung Antonia Candling, her friend, to tell her
that she, Bryony, has been commissioned to edit
a major new poetry anthology.
It's early in the morning and she knows
Antonia will be jealous – quite rightly.

'Darling, it's Bryony,' she begins brightly,
but an answering silence warns her and she decides
best for the moment to withhold her news.
After more silence, in a voice 'duller
than fog, gunked-up with tears, sludgy
with grief' – as Bryony will later put it

in her journal, her book of debit and credit,
where her dealings with the world, daily and nightly,
are entered without permission or apology
for the world to read later – Antonia 'recites
her woes'. Bernard has died. '*Ipsum dolor
sit amet*,' Bryony thinks, though God knows

where that Latin wafted in from, and she knows
better than to say it out loud. Oops, she's said it!
Antonia's silence grows stiller,
loftier, more remote, while Bryony lightly
changes tack and in one gush proceeds
to improvise a perfect Bernard eulogy.

Lucky she's an expert on elegy –
theme of the book that should have been her big news.
Thus, in the tit-for-tat of friendship, both sides
stand even; and Bryony's still in credit
by one unused surprise. They disengage politely.
'Thank you, my dear.' *'Courage.'* 'Will try.' 'Till the . . .'

Ordinary phone silence, this time. Now who to tell the
two stories to: Antonia's loss and her own anthology?
Of course, Derek Dufton! Her forefinger is sprightly
on the keypad. This should put Derek's nose
nicely out of joint. Unless he's heard it
already. Doubtful. That tortoise. Besides . . .

Two ～

I
—

B ryony Butters scans and counts the mourners
gathered to pay their last respects to Bernard
in the small North London church he never attended,
a crowd of types who barely noticed him
when alive, now all agog for his ashes and dust.
Leonard Filcher, next along, whispers: 'You're joking.

A man of his age and condition, out jogging?'
'It's true,' she says. He sighs camply: 'Madness!
Running away from Antonia and her good taste,
I dare say. How could he have borne it,
cooped-up in that colour-supplement home
of theirs? Small wonder if he was tempted to end it.'

'Splendid turn-out,' Bryony says. 'Oh, yes, splendid.'
Poets and civilians are still jockeying
for pew-space, not all of them,
it must be recorded, showing the nicest of manners.
Antonia herself, in a veil-swathed black bonnet,
waits calmly up front, enduring the test

of public grief with perfect composure: a tacit
reproof to Bernard's two sisters, who have surrendered
to base emotion, abandoned
all restraint, and are now crumpled and shaking
with huge sobs. The organ's vox humana is
going a bit strong, too. Identifying the hymn

that's being worked-over, Bryony starts to hum,
then remembers and stops. These are the oddest
occasions, aren't they? More comedies of manners
than rites of ultimate solemnity. The organ has wandered
into an uncharted key and is fumblingly seeking
its way back, when – shades of the boneyard –

the coffin arrives: four scowling men with Bernard
shelved on their shoulders. But that can't be him!
It's a fraud, a con-trick! Preposterous! Shocking!
Why doesn't somebody jump up and protest?
Open the box, for pity's sake, up-end it
and set him free! But on and on the organ maunders.

2

Charles Prime has chosen to skip the churchy bits,
preferring to catch up at the reception.
He's not been invited – but be fair, a man must eat.
Things have been tough, though at last he's found a place
to stay: a photographer friend's studio flat,
borrowed in the hope that the occasional fashion model

might drop round. Only there's been a muddle:
the friend is a war photographer. Still, it beats
sleeping on floors and sofas and having to flit
from one billet to the next. At the reception,
there's plenty to guzzle and gulp, plus
several old flames Charles is not displeased to meet:

Antonia herself, Bryony, a few others. 'Sweet
girl,' he says to Antonia, 'you deserve a medal
for bravery.' 'Charles, what are you doing here?' she replies.
'Widow-chasing,' he tells her, between bites.
'In that nasty tweed jacket?' His pleasantry's barbed reception
delights him: it takes two to flirt,

and he leers at her over the rim of his champagne flute.
But that's his ration. Time to retreat,
pour mieux sauter later. By now the reception
is thinning out. Who next? Flo's in the middle
of a tête-à-tête, Miranda's looking distinctly bats,
so it has to be Bryony: 'Come back to my palace?'

Wild opening shot – but it works! 'Say "please".' 'Please.'
Within an hour, they're at the Bayswater flat,
with brandy glasses and a saucer for cigarette butts
between them. 'You seem to have fallen on your feet,'
Bryony remarks. Charles pulls a non-committal
face. 'Could be. But Christ, I had no conception

how London's changed – with the blessed exception
of the dear old Eagle. What's happened to the place?
If it no longer wants me, well, frankly, the feeling's mutual.'
'Are you sure', Bryony asks, 'it's London's fault?'
He contemplates this. 'Could you repeat . . . ?
No, don't. Don't bother. Just come here and kiss me, Butters.'

3

Jane Steep is using her night off to attend
a poetry reading at the Old Knacker's Yard
in Islington. That's north of the river,
terra incognita, land of fable.
The maze of her map and iffy directions from several
men who do wear their heads beneath their shoulders,

but know the lie of the land no better than she does,
almost persuade her to drop the attempt;
then there it is, bang in front of her, after all.
£5 entry: more than she can afford –
but hey! She takes an aisle seat; a certifiable
scruff takes the one behind; she moves over.

The MC's jokey intro goes on forever,
before the illest assortment of poets – mumblers and shouters,
shamblers and strutters – bring their variable
party tricks to the mic. To get her ear attuned
to the medley of voices, Jane shuts eyes and frowns hard.
Words crash down on her like a waterfall.

What does it mean, she wonders, this free-for-all
of self-advertisement, none of it moving or clever?
While glad not to be spending the evening on guard
against Kurdish Dave, among the flames and shadows
of Sunny's kitchen, she can't pretend
that this is much fun. In fact, it's a form of verbal

torture. One figure rises above the general burble:
a pony-tailed popinjay, very full
of himself, but whose verses are sometimes well-turned
and may even make sense. In a fever
of shyness, she approaches him. 'Hi,' she dares,
'I really liked your villanelle thing.' He looks bored,

extracts from his inside pocket a business card
and pushes it at her. Unbelievable!
She wants to say something apropos, but the shutters
are already down and he's back to the waffle
and tattle of his friends. Did you ever . . . ?
Staring at the card, not reading it, she's stumped, stunned.

4

Antonia Candling finds that, in the low days
following the funeral, literary chores
help to keep her mind distracted.
Now's the time to catch up on her reading
for the big anthology she's been asked to compile:
appropriately, a book of elegies.

By nature neat and decisive, she enjoys
rounding up and grading the thousand threnodies
of past and present. Already there's a generous pile
of rejects; a smaller one, where the choice
is pending a second, more exacting reading;
then a smaller one still, of the unrejected.

Poems go weak in the knees as they wait to be inspected.
Even the nation's best-loved laments and dirges
may have to submit to a new, low rating
at the hands of this editor. Nobody's
feelings are to be spared in her court of justice,
where there is no appeal.

Antonia's on to the Ps now: Patmore, Peele,
Pitter, Pope, Praed, and then – not unexpected,
yet requiring the most delicate handling – Charles
Prime, whose 'Church Bells', a sub-religious
farewell to his mother and a tritely melodious
exercise in self-pity, she remembers him writing

in a poky hotel room, just outside Reading,
as the eponymous bells 'Spilt and splashed a full peal /
Into the close summer air'. This modest
twelve-liner, by a writer of no eminence, owes its protracted
life to the charity of one or two anthologies.
If she left it out of hers, would it look churlish?

Antonia's rattled, of course, by Charles's
capricious reappearance. Shouldn't he be rotting
in gaol? The culpable leniency of our judges!
Thought of his being at large again turns her pale:
the resurrection man resurrected
and on the prowl for fresh bodies.

5

Derek Dufton puts his hand on Gail's knee
and instantly knows he's made a mistake.
Her glaze of prettiness cracks; she discolours; tears
bulge from her eyes. 'Dr Dufton!' 'Gail, stop, I'm sorry . . .'
But she's snatched up her bag and left the room,
heading, he imagines, for the Vice-Chancellor's office.

He sits, feeling sick, while on his desk two coffees,
almost touching, grow cold. The agony
of impotent regret! Though he'd meant no harm,
merely wished, with a gentle pat or stroke,
to comfort Gail, whose deep, if unspoken, sorrow
had appealed so powerfully to his . . .

No, that won't wash. He's simply lost it; worse,
lost it and gained nothing; like Orpheus,
who let the girl slip, then was torn to shreds, he thinks sourly.
Could be a poem in that? He's not written any
poetry for a while, aside from the odd distich,
haiku, or mid-meeting epigram,

and might welcome the sack, if it returned him to his old form:
sometimes a poem a day for stretches, even twice
daily – and there's an impressive stack
of not-so-slim volumes, if you want proof of this.
That would be a satisfactory irony,
and the break he's been waiting for, surely?

He has half a mind to go to the VC and casually
confess to the misdemeanour. Well, erm . . .
perhaps not. What would he do for money?
The reviews he writes for that Sunday culture-rag – terse,
trenchant, Olympian models of critical artifice –
pay less than you might think. So he's stuck.

Or is he? His sleep problem – stark
awake most nights, narcoleptic by day – is a real misery
and could be used in defence. That's it: he's off his
chump! Barmy! A bad dose of teaching-load barm!
Good as a year's sabbatical, if he can show the doctors
that this Gail business was just him going a bit funny.

6

Jonathan Wilderness has looked everywhere
twice, three times, for his quarry, without luck.
The author of *Night Flights* and *A Souvenir
of Soho* is proving as hard to find as his own books –
a second damned elusive Pimpernel!
Yet the hunter refuses to be discouraged;

on the contrary, he's actively encouraged
by something faint but acrid in the air,
the whiff of diablerie and charnel
that rises from certain Charles Prime poems. Look
at these lines: 'Let our sweet error in a deep box /
Lie crossed and cursed, / And nobody come near!'

Some unspecified guilt? Shame? Paranoia?
Whatever, the rhetoric in which it's couched
reeks of secrecy and wrong. Unless it's pure word-bollocks . . .
No, there's definitely something going on here,
and you don't drop a murder case simply for lack
of a corpse, do you? It's the poetry that's in denial,

not the reader. All the more reason to nail
the poet, apt as he is to slip into thin air
ten seconds before you've got him in an arm-lock.
'Just left, mate. Said he was going to church!'
'Really?' 'Yeah, he's joined the choir.'
Despite false trails, wrong turns and stumbling-blocks,

Jonathan keeps searching. He baulks
at no long shot, flagging only when the infernal
harem, the girl gang, back home begins to wear
at his stamina: no-clothes Mimi, tempestuous Lavinia,
Cath the Goth, Nancy who's always crouched
at the end of his bed when he wakes up – like

he needs it! Increasingly, he'd like
to escape. Right now, as it happens, the thought evokes
that mouse at the Knacker's, with the crocheted
scarf, who impressed him when she remarked on his villanelle.
Why hasn't he heard from her, or seen her?
Didn't he give her his card a week ago? Queer . . .

Three ❧

I

Jonathan Wilderness, alongside his pursuit
        of Charles Prime, has been dashing around London
on various errands no less urgent.
His general purpose being to fly the flag
of his genius as conspicuously as possible,
he's like a puppy with his first erection.

By sheer push, he's gained an introduction
to the great Bill Gubney, in whose Thamesside suite
he's attempting to look both brilliant and humble,
as Gubney dishes out the lowdown:
'Poetry? I'd rather try to flog
bottled piss from a stall outside a gents!'

This is Jonathan's first meeting with a literary agent,
a type unlikely to tolerate contradiction.
'Of course,' he says, with a nod and a flick
of his pony-tail; he can see what's what,
and, even as his heart feels increasingly leaden,
he knows he's going to have to play ball.

Before he can slip in, 'Mr Gubney . . .', or even, 'Bill . . .',
his host is booming again: 'You seem an intelligent
young fellow, in spite of your hair-do. Listen:
forget your rhymes, scrap the entire collection.
Wake up! Get a life!' Jonathan is beginning to sweat
wretchedly. But then there's a flicker

of hope: 'This old has-been Soho figure,
whatsisname: if he's the real deal and no bull,
I reckon I could get you a sweet
advance on that one. A little more diligent
sniffing and digging, closer inspection
of the shameful secrets, the soiled linen . . .'

Well, every clown, they say, has a silver lining,
and Jonathan's almost grateful to this fat flake
as he shakes hands with him. The connection,
however, will be purely financial. Double
standards? No! Simply the expedient
of a creative artist obliged to get by on his wits.

2

Bryony Butters says, 'I don't see why
you're running away from him.' Charles Prime says,
'Lifelong habit.' 'But you don't know what he wants.'
'He wants to meet me. That's sinister enough.'
Bryony says, 'What if he's a publisher
who admires your work?' Charles does his snarling laugh.

'Well,' she says, 'I suppose it's your life
to ruin as you choose.' And, breasts asway,
she's up and by the bed. 'I shan't try to put pressure
on you.' 'You couldn't,' Charles says,
adding: 'You know, you're not bad in the niff,
for a woman of your years.' With a wince,

she looks down at herself. 'I was gorgeous once.
Do you remember when we were madly in love?'
'Were we?' Charles says. Stifling a sniff,
Bryony dresses hastily. Then she's away
to the world of daylight and doing that Charles seldom sees.
It's raining, in steady, London style, and still rush hour,

but Bryony's excited by a new idea. She's not sure
if it's a journal entry, or if it warrants
knocking into verse, and her mind seesaws
between the alternatives. The theme is love.
The thrust: she'd like to take his sinewy
old heart and slice it with a kitchen knife . . .

By the time she's reached Clapham North,
the heart has been a toad at leisure
in a stagnant puddle; a sodden tennis ball; a dog's chewy
toy, all beslobbered; a dying rat; a leathery quince
in need of sugar and slow cooking; a stale loaf;
and a few things besides: an excess

of metaphor, which she must seize
ruthlessly, and more than enough
to keep a sequence of twelve unrhymed sonnets alive.
At home, the words mass on-screen, without erasure
or revision. No reason to stop and question the whence
or the whither, and certainly not the why.

3

Derek Dufton reads, 'Thanks for the review
and all that you've done for us over the years.
I hope you won't be disappointed to learn . . .' –
that he's been axed! They've taken on someone younger:
'more in touch with the literary tastes
of our target readership'. By which they mean teenagers!

Alert to the approach of one of his futile rages,
Derek shuts both eyes, bides a few
minutes, breathing deeply, then copies, pastes,
saves, and files the affront. Keeping dossiers
on such incidents helps him to manage his anger
somewhat. Now he paces his flat like a roused lion.

Goes without saying, he's used to standing alone
against the massed artillery of outrageous
fortune. The Gail saga, for instance: the longer
he's made to wait for that still-unscheduled interview
with the VC, the plainer it appears
that he's being put through some kind of test –

if you can call psychological torture a test.
The fake madness ploy, he's decided, was the wrong line,
so he's dropped it; but now he fears
being driven to the real thing by the egregious
sadists in Admin. They're the invisible foe.
Well, let time tell who's the stronger . . .

His pulse is speeding, skittery as a bongo.
Should he take a pill and lie down? The other wrist's
just as jumpy. Better stop prowling. Phew!
There are times when his own body seems an alien
place to be living, as unfriendly and dangerous
as any of the raw demographic frontiers

he's pitched camp close to over the years
since his divorce. From this very window in Katanga
Road, he's seen his quota of gang rampages,
muggings, drug deals, shake-downs and arrests.
Talking of which: there, at the corner of Edge Lane,
something's up, for which he has the perfect view.

4

Charles Prime is well aware that his visit
will be half-expected, so, to turn the moment
back to his advantage, he has chosen
ten in the morning as the hour to press
Antonia Candling's antique, porcelain doorbell.
She's more disconcerted than she lets herself look.

'Don't stand there giving me that smug look,'
she says. 'Come in. And move fast,
before the sunlight kills you.' 'You know, you're adorable',
Charles says, 'when you're pissed-off. One moment!'
Swinging a sports-bag and not bothering to suppress
an even bigger smirk, he marches in.

Soon, they're face to face in Antonia's kitchen.
'After a bad patch,' he says, 'I feel my luck
may be on the up.' There's brandy in his espresso –
'Certainly beats a prison breakfast' –
which emboldens him further: 'This could be a permanent
arrangement, don't you think?' She's imperturbable,

or makes a brave shot of seeming imperturbable,
as the case requires all her cunning and caution.
'Excuse the muted quality of my merriment,'
she says. 'But you've often reminded me that I lack
a sense of humour.' 'Nor have I revised
my opinion. You're still the Empress

of Iceberg to me.' And with such thrusts and parries
the exchange continues, intimate and terrible,
till, by degrees, Antonia is forced
against the wall and the upshot of the discussion
is that she'll take him in. 'Though lock
and key suited you better,' is her final comment,

to which he replies, insouciantly: 'No comment.'
He's gentleman enough, though, not to want to embarrass
her more than need be. After all, how will things look
to the world? Adding a last drip of coffee to his treble
brandy, he says: 'Tell people I'm your cousin
from Woolloomooloo, or somewhere, on an extended visit.'

5

Antonia Candling bumps into Bryony Butters
at the do for Leonard Filcher's new magazine,
Umbilicus. 'Have you any idea',
Bryony asks, 'where Charles Prime has got to?'
'Back in prison?' Antonia suggests, then changes the subject:
'Is there any real difference between a launch

party and a lynch mob?' 'Have you been at a lynching?'
Bryony wants to know, but, as Antonia flutters
for the answer, Leonard himself interjects.
A young man with a somehow obscene
bald head looms behind him. 'Ladies, you've got to
meet my new discovery. The Filcher radar

picked him up at once. You've no idea
how talented! Think of the young Lawrence
Durrell. I'll leave him with you. You'll have a lot to
talk about.' The young man mutters
his name – Jonathan Something – says he's seen
and admired their new poems, modestly rejects

their praise of his (not read either), and starts to explain his project.
Ah, really? Yes, but ages ago. Poor dear,
quite forgotten now. The old Soho scene,
who wants to know about that? Well, could do lunch,
though there's little to tell . . . The young man almost stutters
with gratitude, as they find an escape route to

the far end of the room. Each wonders if they ought to
join forces against this menace, but then rejects
the notion; in fact, neither utters
a word; you're on your own, when there's a literary bash to endure;
and isn't it rather late for an alliance?
Instead, they kiss goodbye. 'Mwa!' 'See you soon!'

By the end of the party, Antonia has seen
one prize-winning poet fall to the floor, blotto;
a second make an ineffectual lunge
for a third's girl; a fourth address a fifth with insulting adjectives;
and a sixth being sick. How she longs to slam the door
on this whole world of nasties, nuisances, nincompoops and nutters!

6

Jane Steep has lost her job, in circumstances
too mad and speeded-up to recall clearly.
Several days later, she is still trying hard to fit
remembered pieces of the story together.
Writing it down, which she thought might help a little,
turns out to be as baffling an exercise

as writing a poem. She drops her pen and sighs.
The phrases sit on the page with enormous distances
between them and no amount of fiddle
can join them up. A mind-map, tried earlier,
came out looking like a chart of yesterday's weather
in Hell. How can she make sense of any of it?

What is clear is that Kurdish Dave, in a fit
of either lust or loathing – she can't be more precise,
but he must have been at the end of one tether
or the other – went for her with a knife. The evidence is
under a medical dressing now, nagging sorely.
Dave himself is laid-up in hospital.

The oddest thing, the inexplicable middle
part of the narrative, is how the stumpy and unfit
figure of Dr Dufton entered the fray, cavalierly
snatching the knife off Dave – who must be twice his size –
and turning it on him. As one of 'Dufton's dunces',
Jane suffered hours of his pedagogical blether,

so recognised him at once, while wondering whether
she might be hallucinating; but, as Dave toppled like a skittle
and Dufton adopted one of his lecture-room stances,
as if to say 'QED!', the photofit
became the real thing: three-dimensional and life-size.
Paying no attention to Jane, he stood squarely,

until the spinning lights and hurly-burly
of the emergency services. Jane, in a dither,
was led away by medics, but saw the police seize
Dufton and push him into a van, more than a little
spitefully: just one item from a surfeit
of nonsense impressions, weirdly disjunct instances . . .

Four ❧

I

J ane Steep has roused herself to make enquiries:
   Dr Dufton has been been up before the magistrates
and is now out on bail; the University,
however, can tell her nothing of his whereabouts,
claiming indeed to be unaware of his absence.
Her only option is to go back to Katanga Road

and find which house in that poor, drab, traumatised road
he emerged from. Not the least curious
aspect of all that makes so little sense
to her is the matching of Dr Dufton with a street
like this: such an improbable habitat
for a man of his high moral tone and sensitivity.

But that's London all over, bewildering city –
as difficult as late Henry James to read!
Jane's first, experimental buzzes and rat-a-tats
are answered, if at all, by blank stares or curses,
but, before she's tempted to beat a retreat,
a chained door quarter-opens and she senses

her old teacher behind it. His continued silence is
problematic, though, as is his invisibility.
'Dr Dufton?' Her voice betrays a note of entreaty.
'Dr Dufton!' Better. 'I hope it's not rude,
but this is Jane Steep. I took one of your courses:
Victorian Pre-Modernism. But that's

not why I'm here.' Her heartbeat's
in her throat and each wrong-angled sentence is
liable to take her further off course,
if she can't get a grip on her unaccustomed loquacity.
Try again: 'Dr Dufton, I don't wish to intrude,
but actually you saved my life.' There: out straight!

Well, straightish. He doesn't appear straight-
away, but two minutes later, or thereabouts,
after much chain-disentangling, he steps out, red-
eyed and rumpled, into daylight, stares, or squints,
at his visitor, then embraces her with rapacity
and gives her a long, fierce, intimate kiss.

2

Jonathan Wilderness is enjoying a rare taste
of real, cooked food as Bryony Butters's guest
at Le Cochon Farci, in deepest Fitzrovia.
Bryony is in plain-speaking mode:
'You must do something about that hairstyle of yours:
it makes you look like an undernourished bouncer.'

Rather than giving a defensive answer,
Jonathan nods his assent. Being told-off and teased
by this voluptuous woman of twice his years
is strangely fun. And who would have guessed
a week ago that he would have made
such progress? Across the table sits an actual lover

of Charles Prime's! But will she hand over
the goods? Lay the charm on, and the chances are
she will. Meanwhile, this *mousse de crevettes au vermouth*
is the heavenliest thing he has ever tasted
and he shovels it into his face with gusto.
When Bryony says, 'I suppose you could use

a little inside help with this book of yours,'
he nods again, his mouth full of steak *au poivre*,
then registers a gentle pressure against
his inside leg. He stops chewing. Does she think he fancies her?
Does he? *Please!* Yet to protest
that he's unavailable, or not in the mood,

would scarcely further his endeavour. It would be mad,
in fact. So, gulping down steak, he says, 'Yes,
I could use some help.' Bryony's toast
is 'To our collaboration and your great oeuvre!'
With a jink of glasses they solemnise the venture,
and 100 ml of Château Auguste

is sent down to settle in Jonathan's troubled guts.
Bryony herself continues in frolicsome mood
all the way home to Clapham. 'Isn't this what friends are
for?' she asks; and, once more, what can he say but 'yes',
as he lets her pull off his pullover,
whooping and tickling him when it gets in a twist?

3

Antonia Candling is fast beginning to tire
of the presence of her self-invited lodger.
Not that she sees much of him: his waking hours
and hers seldom coincide,
his habits being predominantly of the night.
Yet she feels him as a constant burden.

In the first place, he isn't dear old Bernard,
for whom she continues to shed a punctual tear;
an unpunctual one, too, when she catches sight –
or the sight catches her – of some object, large or
small, that was his: his diary, his suede
driving-gloves, the clippers he used on his nasal hairs.

The traces Charles leaves behind him in the house
are another torment: the deathly, burnt
pong of his cigarettes; the loo not flushed; suds
speckled with bristles at the bottom of the basin; an entire
box of stuffed dates scoffed; puddlings of lager
on the kitchen floor; a stove-ring left alight . . .

It's hard to remember, in this light,
that he was the first of her poetic heroes,
who stirred in her a vision of her own larger
potential and to whom she remains beholden –
well, for a number of reasons. *The Gaunt Tower,*
her first book, called 'formidably assured'

by James McDodd, wasn't, in Charles's absurd
phrase, 'ghost-written', but she did learn from him how to write
a few of the weaker and less mature
poems in it. No need to rehearse
old arguments again. Subject *verboten*!
That particular page of the ledger

is doubly underlined. But now, as non-paying lodger,
Charles is collecting other debts – sod
him! Irrationally, she blames her departed husband
for leaving her in this plight.
Oh, Bernard, how could you . . . ? But then she hears
a key fretting at the front door. Time to retire.

4

Bryony Butters has dropped in on her editor
at Rumbold and Furlong, in Howland Square.
She has her anthology with her, done and dusted.
'That was impressively quick work,' he remarks,
speed-reading through the contents list:
'I see it's very much "the nation's favourites".'

'Why not let the nation fall for its
favourites all over again?' He nods at her:
'Quite right. And Sales will love it. Now let's
find something to eat.' Over her moussaka,
Bryony dangles a lure that makes
her editor lay down his fork, hawkishly interested.

'Robert, you know I've always trusted
you absolutely.' She pauses; let him wait for it;
which he does, as titillation must precede climax
and, in all the years he has served as her editor,
she has never let him down on that score.
When she comes out with it at last,

there is a pause of his own, to show that he's lost
for words, then: 'Bryony, "interested"
barely begins . . . This will be the literary shocker
of the decade . . . But can we pay you enough for it . . . ?'
And so on: the sort of author–editor
schmooze-session that every outsider mocks,

but is precisely what fuels the engine that makes
the world of books spin round. So let's at least
let them get on with it. Whether you applaud it or
not, such are the industry's tried and tested
methods, and no amount of huffing or puffing over it
will render its internal workings less obscure.

Let us, rather, seek out, identify and skewer
the world's more pernicious moral murks,
and avoid the temptation to belabour its
minor peccadilloes, lest,
when humankind is done and dusted,
our own books are thrown out by the ultimate auditor.

5

Charles Prime shouts at the Eagle's barman:
'Have you seen the bugger with the pony-tail
who used to be after me all the time?'
'Pony-tail? Oh, him. He lost his hair all of a sudden.
Nah, not shown his face for over a week.'
Charles feels disconcertingly let down.

The truth is, he has scarcely a friend in town –
if you discount a dozen or so women –
and he's grown almost fond of this pestering pipsqueak
he's never even seen. Having him on his tail
was a form of companionship, added a certain
kick to his daily squandering of time.

Life's big mystery, what to do with time –
dull stuff that gushes from a tap you can't turn
off – has him totally beaten,
as does the whole, supposedly noble, human
enterprise, which for most people seems to entail
a life-sentence of unremitting work.

He's recently had his own taste of work:
the daft chores they inflict on you when you're doing time!
Yes, he knows what he's talking about, in detail,
and it stinks. They get you up at some hour called dawn,
then chivvy you non-stop. You're treated like vermin.
Do this, do that! And the other's forbidden!

So here's a lesson that won't be forgotten:
whatever our life on earth is about, work
isn't it. Can't be. Yet the common
alternatives – standing about till closing-time
and seeing how much you can drink without falling down;
throwing your pocket money at the gee-gees; chasing tail –

don't stack up either. As for the tall tale
of poetry, which promised to reveal all hidden
secrets; the irrepressible little tune
that, once started, would chirrup away like clockwork
till a poem was on the page . . . ? Mists of time!
Harder to catch these days than the eye of a barman.

6

Derek Dufton's surprise rediscovery
of his poetic gift happens one morning
as he sits at his computer, thinking of Jane Steep.
Is the connection between these two things causal?
Could she be his Muse? He hasn't, on the whole,
given much credence to theories of the Muse

and anyway doubts if a creature so like a mouse –
slight, shy, scurrying, nervy –
could bear the weight of that imperious role.
Yet he won't hastily dismiss the possible meaning
of their encounter. There was nothing casual
about their one afternoon of sex: the slow, steep

ascent to fulfilment that seemed to answer a deep
want in each of them. Or so he presumes.
He never enquired. And that was his last, actual
sight of her. She made her departure very
promptly after a third, thrashing and moaning
orgasm. 'Goodbye, Dr Dufton,' was her whispered farewell.

Just as puzzling, the manner of his renewal:
the poems come almost too fast to be typed,
in unfamiliar voices and styles, a mounting
glossolalia. Perhaps it's not a Muse
but the Holy Spirit that's guiding him through this reverie?
Or is the fount of poetry always sexual?

His old stuff now strikes him as contemptibly intellectual:
cautious, prissy, horribly well-
groomed. Why did he once believe that every
poem had to be so clean, so stripped
of all trace of its human origin, so anonymous?
Never mind that: no point in mourning

what's been lost, when a new, commanding
force is urging him forward. The crucial
thing is to keep bashing on, while the Muse –
or whoever – has him under her will,
directing him to take risks, to overstep
rational limits, to exult in his own crazy bravery . . .

Five ❦

I

Derek Dufton – unwittingly, of course –
will secure a place for himself in the *oxbridge
ecyclopedia of 21c verse*
+ *nonverse* with the outpourings of this period.
'Dufton,' the electronic scholar will write,
'about whose later life little is known,

may be credited as begetter of the Non-
verse revolution, changing the course
of poetry with a paperbook he is said to have written
in less than a month: *The Silence of the Ostrich
Is More Terrible than the Song of the Parrot*
(2015). Eschewing the orthodox verse

line, its 200 pages set out to reverse
almost every practice of an outmoded canon
and led to such achievements of the present period
as the work of the Foul Mouthers, the School of Chaos,
and the Logorrhaeologists centred on Oxbridge.'
He will go on to compare Dufton's writing

with the visions of Bosch and the automatic writings
of the Surrealists, only granting Dufton the greater force:
'A thirty-page invocation – "Goddess! Dog's bitch!"
et cetera – caps noun with noun
in a frenzied crescendo. Quite whom this curse
is directed at is not apparent,

but the effect is that of a wholesome aperient
allowing the release of some of the "foulest" writing
ever set down, a perfect example of deranged discourse,
or what the French call *écriture féroce.*'
Certainly, when Derek first reads from its pages, no one
listening is prepared for such a rich

effluence of gibberish.
Antonia Candling whispers, 'Is it a parody?'
Bryony Butters whispers back, '*J'ai peur que non.*'
And they spend the next hour writhing.
Jane Steep is there too. Seated as far as
possible from the podium, she shuts both eyes and cowers.

2

Jane Steep is trying hard to follow
as the large and lumpily uniformed policewoman
explains the latest developments. It seems
Kurdish Dave has done a runner from hospital,
in fact left the country, so now they're dropping
all charges against Dr Dufton.

The WPC speaks gently, as if to soften
the news. She's like a kindly buffalo,
Jane thinks, her mind scattily hopping
from one thought to the next; then she summons
her concentration to ask, 'Is that all . . . ?
I mean . . .' But the words swim

out of reach. 'So am I . . . ?'
Her eyes search the ceiling. The WPC, who has often
had to deal with the dazed and brittle
condition of witnesses, says, 'Forget the fellow,
he won't come near you. Woman to woman,
they're all mouth and self-service, that sort. Won't be stopping

round this borough, anyhow. Galloping
for the hills, more like. Right, Jane, I assume
I can leave you . . . ?' Jane feels an immense
feebleness preventing her from mentioning Dr Dufton
and the fears about him she's full of now.
Since his acquittal, or what amounts to acquittal,

what weight would her flimsy tittle-tattle
about his mad rant carry? Does chopping
a person's head off in reality necessarily follow
from the menacing metaphors in some –
fuck, was it a poem? Answer me that, Dr Dufton,
you who once taught and examined me on

'Porphyria's Lover'! But neither he nor the policewoman
is there to reply. Perhaps a little
lie-down, then. It's early afternoon;
outside the window some whopping
machine is pounding and pulverising paving-stones; yet slumber
comes as soon as she hugs her pillow.

3

Charles Prime has been dragged to the vernissage
of some sort of art show at some sort of gallery
somewhere in East London: absolute shite
on the walls and floor, but so what?
There's drink. And food of sorts. Left to fend
for himself, he's scoffing a canapé

in the form of a tiny, goo-filled pie –
what happened to the good old cocktail sausage? –
when he notices Bryony Butters at the far end
of the róom. *'Que fais-tu dans cette galère?'*
she asks, when he finally reaches her. 'What's that?
I can't hear a word.' They go outside,

light up, and stand side by side,
smoking in silence under the green-tinged canopy
of a London summer evening sky. 'What
wouldn't I give for a decent cocktail sausage!'
Charles says at last. 'Or even a stick of limp celery.'
More silence. Then Bryony asks: 'Who's your little friend?'

'Friend? Oh, her! Tasty, isn't she? And a fiend
between the bedsheets.' 'How old?' 'Just this side
of legal.' 'Unlike me, then,' Bryony says. Golly,
something's up. 'I think I need a pee . . .'
When Charles returns, she's gone. There was a message
in that exchange – but exactly what?

Days later, in the Eagle, he learns what's what.
''Ere, Charlie, good news about your lady friend.'
'Lady friend?' 'Yeah, 'er with the . . .' Old Ted massages
imaginary breasts, then sucks at his cider.
'Go on.' 'Seems she's written 'er autobiography.
Been paid a packet for it. Smart girl, eh?'

A kiss-and-tell job! Then clearly
he'll be in it. So that's what
she was hinting at . . . He dashes to the pee-
sprayed phone-booth down the road, only to find
the apparatus smashed. Now there's a sharp pain in his side.
He really shouldn't be running at his age.

4

Jonathan Wilderness has arranged to meet Baz
at Baz's local. On a tiny, jutting stage,
a lamp-tanned brunette, who has just flung away her thong
with an air of disdain, is lithely twining herself
around a perpendicular pole.
For Jonathan, it's all too much like home.

'Thought you'd fancy a spot of home from home,'
Baz says when he arrives. They sit down with their beers
and crisp packets. 'If you're on the pull,'
Baz whispers, 'I need to warn you, she's under age.'
Jonathan glowers at the now upside-down sylph
and shakes his stubbly head: 'Not my kind of thing.

Fact is, right now nothing's my kind of thing.'
He explains how, between the old domestic harem
and the new woman who's adopted him as her sex slave,
he's been run ragged: 'The mere thought of a bare arse
gives me the heebie-jeebies.' 'The wages
of shagging,' Baz opines. 'Man, you look pale.

But if there's anything your old pal . . .'
'Actually,' Jonathan cuts in, 'there is something.'
By the end of a ten-minute huddle, he has engaged
Baz's professional services: 'You're not to harm
her, you understand, just do the business.
Grab it and get out. She thinks it's so safe

where it is, and I can tell you she sleeps like a sloth
after nooky. That'll be me, of course, on the next pillow,
keeping one eye open.' He hands Baz
a plump, brown envelope – 'a little something
on account' – before glancing across the room
to where this new girl, in pinky-beige

knickers and bra, with an ugly bandage
at her shoulder, is clambering on to the dance-shelf.
She looks about her with candid alarm,
the brash light emphasising her pallor
and her goosebumps. When the music starts thumping,
she attempts a few steps, twitchy, embarrassed.

5

Bryony Butters is woken by a sound.
At first, the house pretends nothing has happened,
but listening carefully she knows the silence is false
and – sure enough – there it is again:
a dull thud from downstairs. Jonathan Wilderness
lies beside her, his unbothered head

buried in bedclothes. She shakes him hard,
but he won't be roused. She tries a second
shake: no use. What now? she wonders.
If there's an intruder – not the first time this has happened –
and he (or she) is carrying a knife or a gun,
what could she do? If all else fails,

jump through the bedroom window. She feels
for her precious pendant. Safe! No horrid
burglar, no skunk-righteous, gangland goon,
is going to take that. Then more sounds,
like a scuffle and furniture being up-ended,
and next thing, forgetting her state of undress,

she's at the foot of the stairs in time to witness
a struggling figure she can tell in a flash
is Charles Prime being pinioned
by some young thug in standard-issue hood.
Snatching her knobkerry from the umbrella stand,
she attacks the assailant, lands several blows to the groin,

and it's not long before he's dropped poor Charles with a groan
and left via an open window. 'What a mess,'
Charles says. 'Good thing I was here to sound
the alarm. Any chance of a stiff brandy?' Then he falls
to the floor, his right hand clutching at his heart.
Bryony kneels beside him, meaning to pound

his chest, but there's no point.
As she's rising to her feet again,
she's startled by a voice: 'I thought I heard . . .'
'Oh, it's you. Well, since you're up, Jonathan Wilderness,
Charles Prime, you really should . . .' But she fails
to finish the sentence, for reasons you will understand.

6

Antonia Candling receives the news with aplomb.
She can see herself doing it, just as she can hear
Charles Prime's voice chipping in with 'aplomb in your mouth'.
Her carefully managed self-possession, however,
is really a compound of opposites:
shock at the loss of one close to her and relief

that Charles is now finally out of her life.
The police officer, professionally solemn,
bids her farewell and exits,
leaving her to use as she likes the hours
till dawn. But she can't sleep; can't read; whatever
can she do, with her mind batting like a moth

against incomprehensible light? Not since her mother
died has she felt like this. She mustn't, of course, laugh,
but she can't, in all honesty, weep either.
So she just sits, in an attitude of calm,
while the day arrives in no particular hurry
with all a great, slovenly city's

diffuse waking clatter: traffic, shouts,
birdsong, barking . . . Cometh
the hour, she thinks, goeth the man. Goeth the hour . . .
Man comes and tills . . . until . . . he lies . . . he lieth . . .
asleep. When she opens her eyes, the gloom
of the sitting-room gives her the shivers

even before she recalls the fuss and palaver
of last night. But today's today. Charles's sheets
will need to be washed, the catastrophic slum
of his room cleared out: a mammoth
task that can't be put off, however loth
she may be to venture in there.

Obviously, Mrs Thing won't touch it. So here
goes, with bin-bags and hoover!
By mid-afternoon no trace of Charles is left,
order and propriety have been re-asserted,
and Antonia herself can get on with the smooth
running of her household, her mausoleum . . .

Six ❧

I

Antonia Candling, opening her newspaper
at the obituaries, is disconcerted
to find Charles Prime there. And that old photograph!
But surely he was forgotten long ago –
not by herself, of course, but by the world?
She scans the piece, first, for her own name

(oh, cripes), then for the gist, then for the name
of the writer. Ah, the obsequious whippersnapper
at Leonard's party, the tall, bald boy who hurled
himself at her and Bryony, but whom by concerted
action they chased off. Or so she'd thought. But no.
She folds the paper neatly, with a grave

foreboding. Charles is scarcely in his grave –
and they're digging him up again! In God's name,
why? What's achieved by putting on public show
a life so wasted? Wouldn't it be more proper
to bury the misdeeds with the man? Sordid
business . . . While she's thinking poor old

Charles, and what if they hadn't quarrelled,
the phone rings: it's the *Evening Telegraph*
wanting its bite at the story. All calm is shattered.
'Would you say', the snoop asks, 'that Charles Prime's name
means anything now?' Then: 'Is it true he died a pauper?'
Then: 'You were close at one time, weren't you?' Not slow

to see where this line of interrogation will go
if she doesn't take care, Antonia, though riled,
answers coolly; but you can't block a reporter
even with a great, big banner shouting 'GRIEF!',
and the rag that pays this one has never had a name
for respecting personal feelings. If you try to assert ·

your right to privacy, you'll be sorry you did;
so she doesn't; but an angle occurs to her even so:
'If you do happen to mention my name,
which I don't suppose will be widely known in the world
of your readers, please add that I'm his official biographer.'
Which in the event may not be a complete whopper.

2

'Derek Dufton? Anybody seen Derek?'
Head of Department enquires. Nobody
has. Around the table, Derek's colleagues
present a range of negative facial expressions:
plain 'No', 'Don't ask me', 'Who cares?', even 'Derek who?'
But HoD is now hot on the scent:

'Do the minutes record when he was last present?'
Months ago. 'Look, we need to keep track
of habitual absentees. Not to mention, there've been a few
complaints about Derek from the student body.
Some second-year wants to blame her depression
on his lectures. I know he can be prolix,

though the term she actually used was "complete bollocks".'
General titter of servile assent.
Gratified, HoD says, 'Right, let's press on.
No doubt we can manage without him.' Derek,
meanwhile, is miles away in both body
and spirit. His masterwork finished, he has bidden *adieu*

to poetry, teaching, London, and without further ado
has left town on foot. Days later, bucolic,
Vaughan Williamsy England in all its beauty
rolls around him, a birdsong descant
exults above, and footsore, mildly sunstruck,
stubbled and stinky Derek is a different person:

if not reborn, then sprung from a hideous prison.
Here the fields are green, the sun yellow, the sky blue –
as in a children's book. Why wasn't the trick
of just standing and staring part of his previous knowledge?
Why so long to learn that you don't have to be a saint
to commune with creation? Anybody

can do it. There's a bird in a hedge. Hello, birdie!
Ah, this is the life for him, and no comparison
with the old need shadow it. Derek's descent
of the little hill, in spite of blisters and one gaping shoe,
is rapid; and the spirit of unfettered frolic
keeps him moving at a fair pace until dark.

3

Bryony Butters asks, 'What are you staring at?'
The correct answer is 'your memory stick',
but Jonathan Wilderness can't say that, so he goes,
'Oh, you know . . . your . . . er . . . er . . . your . . .',
then nods as if that were all that need be said.
'Naughty boy,' she replies with a coquettish

simper, then, turning her back, feels for the fetish
that hangs from a chain between her breasts and grips it
tightly. She knows; he knows she knows; how sad
that their delicious fling should be coming unstuck . . .
They dress briskly and in silence. At the front door,
they kiss – peck, peck – and as Jonathan goes

she speeds him on his way with a sly goose
signifying 'adieu', 'no hard feelings' and 'best of British'.
The alliance terminated, why should there be war?
Rivalry, yes, inevitably – but hate?
No way! Still, now's the moment to strike,
while she has the advantage. First, to persuade

Rumbold and Furlong that the contract should
be amended slightly. Robert, the darling, goes
for it at once. Next, to set herself a strict
daily timetable and word-count – or strict-ish:
a sustainable balance of fine writing and white heat,
possibly three thousand words per day, no more.

She begins that very afternoon. Words pour
steadily on to the screen. Having shed
all demureness, or what remained of it,
Bryony finds that she has the power to gaze
straight into her adolescence: those callow, skittish,
brash and venturesome years. Historical

research – and all done without her memory stick!
(Isn't that what our memories are for?)
Look, there she is, gawky and puppy-fattish,
and there's Charles Prime, the famous poet, said
to be a danger to innocent, unripe girls.
He smiles at her. So that's what they were driving at!

4

Jane Steep is gradually getting used
to her new job. Job? All right, how else
would you describe it? 'Dancing naked
in a pub' may never feature on her CV,
but there's reasonable money at the end of a stint
and it leaves her time to write. Theoretically.

At first treated less than sympathetically
by her audience of beery oglers, booed, hissed,
pelted with caveman insults and sick taunts,
she would leave the stage in tears. The malice
of it astounded her. But then a kind and savvy
colleague took her aside – 'No, kid,

you do it like this . . .' – and, while she may be knackered
much of the time, she dances more balletically
than she ever thought possible. It all beats slavery
in Sunny's kitchen, she's grown to like and trust
the girls, and the landlord of this gin palace,
though an ape in the style of Kurdish Dave, keeps his distance.

'Jus' say if 'im, or any bastard, tries a stunt,'
Jazmynne has promised, 'and we'll 'ave 'em nuked . . .'
So Jane feels safe, more or less.
One Friday night, however, she's energetically
bumping and grinding for a house that's largely pissed,
and simultaneously conducting a survey

of facial types, when she's caught by a stab and shiver
of recognition: someone she knows! Knows, but isn't
able to place. Who clearly knows her. The worst!
Discombobulated, knocked
off rhythm, she concludes her dance bathetically
in full panties and bra. The jeering swells

as she jumps offstage, flapping at the air like Alice
attacked by the pack of cards. Somebody save her!
Somebody does: it's Tifni, with the synthetically
contoured boobs, who guides Jane's dazed descent
into their ample haven. 'Now, now, kid,'
she croons, stroking and soothing. Jane rests.

5

Jonathan Wilderness will not give up
his courtship of Jane Steep, despite obstacles.
Barred from the Duke of Hampton, that vile hole,
not by the landlord but by the girls who take
their clothes off there, having learnt Jane's name
through a mate of Baz's, like a troubadour

he sends her a poem a day 'c/o the Stage Door':
villanelles, exclusively. He keeps this up
until the recipient is so numb
from the bombardment, she answers one of his calls
for a truce. They meet in a café. It doesn't take
Jonathan long to convince her he's on the level,

that his intentions, far from being evil,
are pure and poetic: he needs a Muse to adore –
chastely, of course – and she's It. She takes
this in, without comment at first, weighing up
the pros and cons while her coffee cools.
'Chaste?' she asks at last. 'You mean, no . . . um . . . ?'

'Yeah,' he says, 'you got it. That's the norm
with Muses.' 'But why do you want . . . ?' 'Several
reasons' – and Jonathan explains his luckless
domestic predicament: 'I've been a sexual door-
mat to a battalion of nymphos. They won't let up
and it's killing me. If you could just take

me away from all that . . .' Impulsively, he takes
her hand, then drops it at once. No harm
done: she's too deep in thought. 'And I'm to give up
the dancing?' 'Right.' 'OK, I agree.' The hovel
where Jane has her flat is poky, dingy, and open-door
to miscellaneous animal life. Jonathan recoils

when he sees the kitchen: so she's totally clueless
about housekeeping. Could this be a mistake?
But hey – there are worse things to endure,
and he's already bagged his own room
where he can work in seclusion on his novel,
whose narrator, a bad old poet, just won't shut up.

6

Charles Prime: The Poet Remembered,
Antonia Candling's authoritative account,
happens to be published on the same day as
Charles Prime: The Poet I Knew,
Bryony Butters's more intimate memoir.
Although the two books are entirely different,

they carry the same photograph on the front:
the boyish poet seeming to have rambled
in from some lost land of youth, glamour,
wild spirits and high hopes. He holds an ice-cream cornet –
ice-cream eaten – his tie is askew,
his hair is a ragamuffin's thatch, and he looks dazed

by the prospect of a lifetime of bank holidays
threatening never to end. A friend
has linked her arm through his, but we can't tell who,
because she's been cropped. Was it she who rumpled
his hair and loosened his tie? Don't ask questions you can't
answer; leave that to gossip, rumour,

biography – and the press, which immediately raises a clamour:
why do we have to wait till a great poet dies
before we hear of him? And suchlike cant.
The very pundits who were once wholly indifferent
now hail Charles Prime as 'the English Rimbaud',
'a lost Shelley', etc. The hullabaloo

increases when, in a TV interview,
Bryony Butters speaks of her *premier amour*,
then bursts into tears. (Still no one has publicly rumbled
quite what occurred between them.) Within days,
a *Collected Poems* is out from Fuddy and Duddy, frantic
to exploit an author whose sales, when last counted,

barely touched three figures. Then *The Ice-Cream Cornet*,
a scurrilous novel, appears out of the blue:
a blatant *roman-à-clef*, cocky and irreverent.
Loud praise of Charles Prime falls to an irritable murmur,
before fading completely. As soon as it does,
all titles mentioned above are quietly remaindered.